I0787870

Dirt Cheap Prepping:

25 Useful Cheap Stuff To Prepare Now And Use When SHTF

All photos used in this book, including the cover photo were made available under a Attribution-NonCommercial-ShareAlike 2.0 Generic and sourced from Flickr

Copyright 2016 by the publisher - All rights reserved.

This document is geared towards providing exact and reliable information in regards to the topic and issue covered. The publication is sold with the idea that the publisher is not required to render accounting, officially permitted, or otherwise, qualified services. If advice is necessary, legal or professional, a practiced individual in the profession should be ordered.

- From a Declaration of Principles which was accepted and approved equally by a Committee of the American Bar Association and a Committee of Publishers and Associations.

In no way is it legal to reproduce, duplicate, or transmit any part of this document in either electronic means or in printed format. Recording of this publication is strictly prohibited and any storage of this document is not allowed unless with written permission from the publisher. All rights reserved.

The information provided herein is stated to be truthful and consistent, in that any liability, in terms of inattention or otherwise, by any usage or abuse of any policies, processes, or directions contained within is the solitary and utter responsibility of the recipient reader. Under no circumstances will any legal responsibility or blame be held against the publisher for any reparation, damages, or monetary loss due to the information herein, either directly or indirectly.

Respective authors own all copyrights not held by the publisher.

The information herein is offered for informational purposes solely, and is universal as so. The presentation of the information is without contract or any type of guarantee assurance.

The trademarks that are used are without any consent, and the publication of the trademark is without permission or backing by the trademark owner. All trademarks and brands within this book are for clarifying purposes only and are the owned by the owners themselves, not affiliated with this document.

Table of content

Introduction

We never know when nay disaster can hit at our place. We do not have any idea whether we will be able to cope up with the disaster or not. Anything that is cheap now days can become very expensive. It is necessary that we keep some stuff on hand that can be used in time of need. This stuff can also be helpful in any economical crisis. At this moment, it is necessary that we should realize the importance of getting prepared.

It is imperative to note that the items which are cheap nowadays and are available will be very expensive and hard to find. The priceless things become valuable in such instances. It will be very convenient if you want to avoid the nuisance at the last moment as prevention is better than cure. This stuff can be used by you and not only your family, but you can also use it for bartering.

Chapter 01: Cheap Food Items for Prepping

Food stuff is very necessary without which we cannot even think of service. Storing food is a technique and it needs to be wise enough so that we do not run at the eleventh hour. There are many food items that can be stored perfectly, but it needs that we have the right guideline. Here we are discussing some of the ways with which we can store food in an effective way.

1. Canned foods

They have their same importance as does of water. They are the only mean with which you can get the energy to survive. It will give you the nutrients needed by your body. They are the asset for the survival of an individual.

The food stuff is also necessary for giving the required strength that will be helpful for you to walk, ask for help and take measures to escape any calamity. The nutrient will also give you the power to use your brain so that you can think of a perfect plan. There are multiple brands in the market which you can use. Take a look around in the super market and choose the one having longer shelf life and store them.

Make sure to keep multiple number and varieties of canned food. The canned foods can have multiple things. This can be canned meat, canned vegetables, canned fruits, canned pulses and much more. All of the canned foods have longer shelf life and can be used at any time without the need of much cooking.

2. Rice

Rice are full with carbohydrates mainly starch that is one of the instant forms of energy. They will provide you with the quick energy that is needed for doing any work. One of the biggest advantages with the rice is that they can be stored for the longer duration of time. They only need water to get them cooked.

You also do not need to do much with the storage process. They can be cooked easily without the need of many things. If you have multiple options for making rice tasty, you can utilize it. You can easily multiple things to enhance the flavor of the dish which will be nothing more than a piece of heaven in the hour of affliction. You can easily add any broth or soup to enhance the flavor of this rice.

There are many varieties of rice like white rice, brown rice, etc. the advantage with white rice is a longer duration of storage while brown rice has more nutrition. You can store them in a number of sizes and kilograms according to the need of the family.

3. Peanut butter

The advantage with peanut butter is that it has a very good taste and can be used without any cooking at all. They have a lot of protein which is a good source of energy. You can easily feel the energy when you will eat this peanut butter. You can spread it on anything like bread or loaf or can have it as it is. All you need to do is store some of the jars of peanut butter in your home.

Another advantage with the use of peanut butter is that they can be stored for the longer duration of time. You do not need to make many efforts to store it as it had already a number of preservatives that are added. This can be one of the important a delicious addition to the prepress in any case of any emergency and torment.

4. Powdered milk

Powdered milk is used every day in our daily life. These can be added to your stock list to be used in a number of ways. They are dried and can be stored for a couple of days without any hesitation. They are also one of the good sources of energy.

There are many brands that provide with powdered milk. Choose the one that is suitable for your family and like them. You can choose any brand of your choice but make sure that the shelf life is long and it has a longer time to expire.

All you can do is add after to the powder and utilize it without any effort. You can use this powder milk to make a variety of foods like tea, coffee, porridge, rice, etc. They are also very good if you have infants and children in your family. It can be a perfect meal for them in the case of any emergency situation. Children can easily utilize it in the case when you do not have any special products for them to eat.

5. Salt

You must have neglected the importance of salt as it is a very common food present in our homes. In any case of emergency or disaster, this little food becomes priceless. It is the only ingredient which can add significant taste to your food without many efforts.

You will not even be able to find it in any case of disaster and become very expensive. To avoid such situation, it is necessary that you should have plenty of it so that you do not need to run for it. It can significantly enhance the taste of your food.

They do not require any effort to preserve them. The salt can be used to rub it on many things and preserve them like meat, vegetables, etc.

Chapter 02: Cheap Liquids for Your Survival

As the food is necessary, we cannot deny the importance of liquids. They are also very essential for the survival. We might be able to live for a couple of days without food, but it will be very difficult to survive for more than three days without liquids. The liquids are necessary for the survival. They provide us with the essential hydration that can help us use our brain and concentrate.

6. Water

Although water is not in the list of food it is very essential. Water is considered as the most important mineral in the world. Without this, we cannot even think to survive. Keep a number of cans and fill it with pure water. Make sure that the water is pure, and you can drink it. I will be very feasible and good for your health if you will replace this water in the cans on a regular basis with fresh water.

It is crucial to replace this water to fresh that is healthier. You do not want any unhealthy and stale water to store that can affect the health of your family members. You can also buy canned water that can be stored for longer duration without any trouble.

7. Canned liquid

This can be one of the easiest and perfect ways to store liquid which can be used later on in time of need. You can easily stock canned food with high water content. One the example of such food can be canned pineapples. The can contain not only pineapple but also a lot of liquid.

These canned foods will provide food as well hydration for the body. This will help you to prevent depletion of water from the body. You can also add this liquid in cooking that can enhance the taste of the food which you are cooking.

8. Coconut milk

We all know the nutritious value of coconut and coconut milk. Coconuts are rich in minerals and can provide a significant amount of hydration to the body. It not only provides the water but is also loaded with minerals.

You can store this milk and can use in time of need. You can store this in liquid form as well as in powder form. Powder form holds the advantage that it has more shelf-life than the liquid form. The other advantage with coconut milk is that it will help you to cook the rice at a faster pace without much effort.

9. Canned soup

Canned soups can be used for implementation of the life-saving strategy. They are not only delicious but also quite cheap. They also have good storage life and can be used instantly without much cooking. They will give you all the essential nutrients and the hydration required for your body.

You can easily use this soup just by opening it and using it with the help of a spoon. You can also use the broth in cooking other meals like rice without much-needed efforts. This will also add flavors to the food like you can make scrumptious rice by adding the soap into it. This soup can help you to save the pure water which can be used in other cases.

Chapter 03: Cheap Accessories for Your Stock

There are many things which are crucial for our survival. These are not related to food and drinks. These things are counted as extra but can be very fundamental for the survival. They are needed so that we can use them in a time of need.

These items can be used or the shelter or protection. They guarantee our survival and are essential as other things are. Some of these are discussed below:

10. Tents

Tents are not that much expensive. Usually, people who like camping have these in the homes for fun. These can be very important for survival in case of any emergency. Think of any emergency when you do not have any place of survival. At this time you need some place where you can hide and acquire shelter.

These tents are available in multiple sizes and are available with wide range of pricing. You can choose one according to the need of you and your family. These tents can save you from scorching heat, snow, rain and any weather condition. Now a day's many tents are available in compact sizes and can be carried easily.

There are many portable and good quality tents available in the market that can give you the exact protection needed for the survival. They are also tough so can easily bother the wear and tear because of weather.

11. Gasoline

We all know the importance of gasoline in our daily lives. They are used in a very vehicle and running of the machine. It is considered as black gold because of its importance in the global market. The use of gasoline is versatile and has equal importance in the case of any emergency.

It will be very convenient for you and your family to store ample amount of gasoline which you can use later on. This gasoline can be used for any vehicle that you can use to travel to the far and wide place. This can help you to get out of the place of affliction and move to the place which is safe.

On the other hand, if there is no way to get out of the place of torment then simply the gasoline can be used for running of the generator that can provide you with the survival aid needed in a time of need. It will be crucial to store gasoline. You do not need to make much effort to store it. All you need to do is get to the gasoline station and store it in the bottles or can.

Make sure that the gasoline lasts as it has high potential to disappear because it is volatile liquid. Keep on checking the bottles or cans from time to time and refill them when needed.

12. Things that can cut

They are also necessary for the survival quest. These items can include a knife, dagger, ax, or scissors. Usually, these items are used in an everyday household. They are quite helpful and can be a significant help in case of any emergency.

These can be used to cut food and another thing as a rope. They can also be used to cut wood which can be later on use for making food to cook food, provide warmth in the cold and can prevent wild animals to come towards you. They can also be used for protection from harmful human beings and animals.

There can be multiple instances where you need to go somewhere, and any hindrance can prevent your access. You can also use them to dig hole in places where you want to hide or go. These can be the perfect tool for survival.

13. Torch

They are also one of the items that are used quite frequently in the everyday households. They are used in multiple places daily. The advantage of the use of torch is that they are portable to carry and can provide you the significant amount of light needed to see in the dark.

All you need to do is buy a number of torches that are enough according to the need of your family. You also need to check these torches either they are working or not. They can be very useful in case of emergency situations. It can provide you light in every instant you want to.

There are multiple varieties of a torch that are available in the market. There is also variation in the size, warranty, quality and pricing of these torches. You can just pick the one that you find the suitable one for your family. Rely on the high quality of torches as it is the matter of the safety of your family.

14. Tools for communication

These are one of the necessities which cannot be ignored at any cost. There are many sorts of tools that can be used in case of emergency. One of the most basic tools for communication is the mobile phone. We use mobile everyday in our lives. It is the source of fastest and most convenient communication. These mobile phones can be used in case of emergency as well. It will be very convenient if you keep some extra mobile phone with extra batteries.

In a case of emergency, when there is a wide destruction of the infrastructure, the mobile networks may get down. In such cases, the best tools for communication can be a satellite phone, CB radio, HAM radio, and a police scanner and so on.

These are the tools that can be used in case you do not have reception of mobile signals. They cover different ranges and allow you to contact the people for help. The radios work on different frequencies. All of these come in wide variety of types with variable pricing.

Many of the companies are relying on the manufacture of a cheap satellite phone, CB radio, HAM radio, police scanner, etc. you can choose any of it that is sufficient for your need and your family.

15. Batteries

Batteries are present in the everyday household. They are used from toys to phones. The use of batteries is versatile as they are the most convenient and portable source of energy needed for running of different items.

These batteries are also one of the sources that can be used at the time of any emergency. It will be very convenient if you keep some extra batteries at your home. These can be used to run mobile phones, satellite phones or radio. You can help you in contact or provision of vital information needed for an evacuation plan. These can also be used to run torch.

Make sure you have ample number of these batteries and them all working. There are many varieties of batteries available in the market. Some of these have long shelf life. Some of these are specifically designed for disaster management. Choose the battery that has a longer shelf life so that it can be used later on.

Chapter 04: Cheap Medications and First Aid Tools

The disasters are inflicted to a place without any notification. In the same manner, injuries are inevitable in the case of any emergency situation. It will be highly recommended that you have some plans so that you can tackle with any injury.

The best way to deal with such injuries is to take the patient to the hospital where the staff members can treat the patient. In the case, when you do not have any way out to take the patient to the hospital then emergency first aid tools are any source to treat. It is very necessary to know the right guideline with which you can provide first aid to the family members. Here, we will be providing you with some tips to make your emergency Medications and First Aid Tools.

16. Bandages

Bandages are the important part of any first aid kit. They are used to cover the wound so that they kept away from any contamination. They can also be used to stop bleeding. They are the most essential part of the first aid kit.

Keep a number of bandages like 25 to 30 that can be used in any emergency. This much amount is necessary as you may have no idea about the severity of the injury or number of people who can get injured.

There are a number of types of these bandages in the market. All you need to do is to choose bandages of various length and widths that you can use. It is necessary to keep a variety of bandages so that you can have options to use it according to the injury.

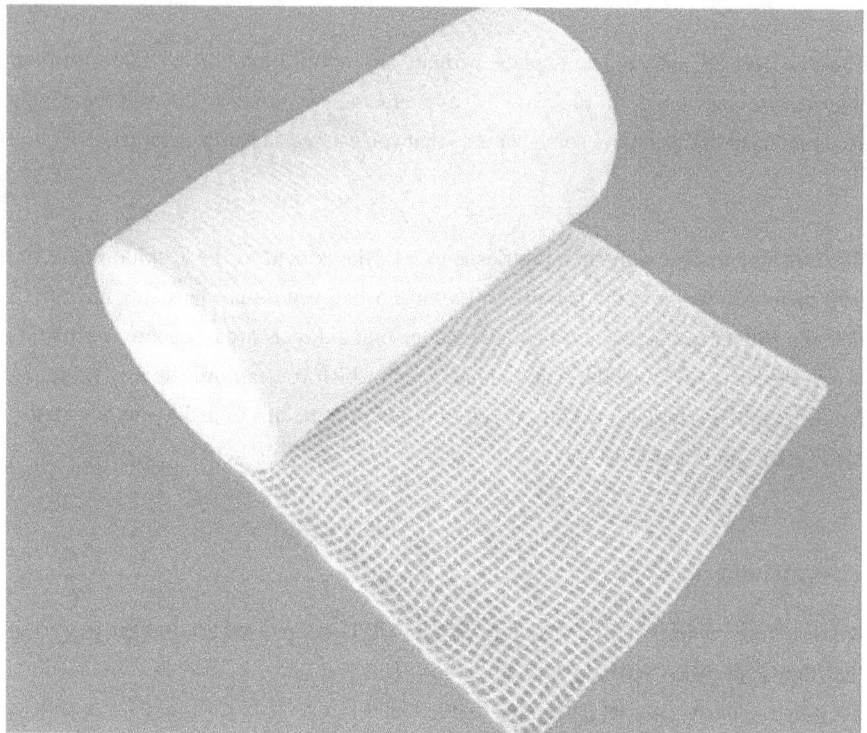

17. Alcohol or alcohol swabs

Alcohol is an antiseptic that can be used to clean the wound. You can either use liquid alcohol or can keep alcohol swab. It will be suggested that you use swabs as in the case of emergency, you may be in panic and may drain a lot of liquid alcohol which can be a waste.

The alcohol swab is already fixed in alcohol and can be used instantly. You also do not need to worry about any cotton or bandage to clean it. There are many brands of alcohol swabs in the market. Choose the one with a longer duration of shelf life.

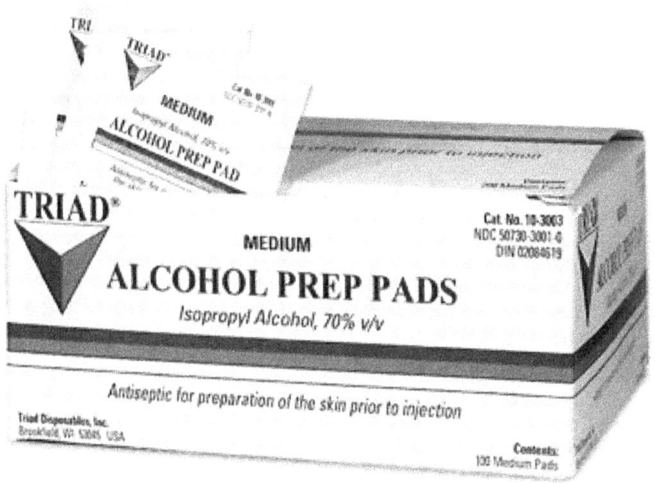

18.Cotton

Cotton is one of the important parts of any first aid kid. The first aid kit is not complete without it. They are used in many emergency situations. It is usually used for cleaning any contamination, cleaning of blood and application of antiseptic or any ointment.

These can be used in any emergency situation in any of the situation described above. They are also available in a variety of sizes and quality. One of the important things with cotton is that you do not need to worry about its shelf life. All you need is to buy it and keep it.

Keep almost 4 to 5 bundles of cotton packs or according to the need of the family. Buy cotton that has the good absorbent ability and can be used to soak a lot of material so that you do not need to run in the hour of need. It is also imperative that you keep packed cotton packs for the emergency first aid kit so that the cotton does not get contaminated.

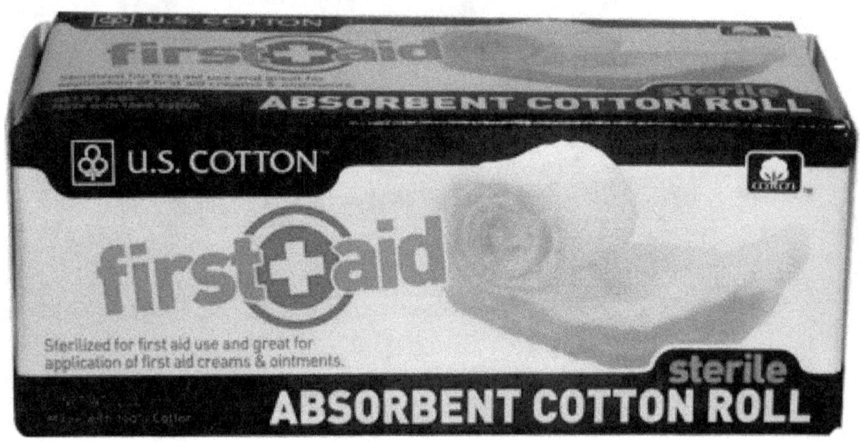

19. Pain killers

Pain killers are used to helping us tolerate and get rid of the pain. The most common used pain killer is paracetamol. It is the drug which is present over the counter and can be bought in a time of need. Pain killers are present in every house hold, and they are very effective in treating the painful condition.

They are also very important in the emergency situation. There may be conditions when any of the family members may get injured. Although, you might have covered the bleeding and all but the pain may disturb the injured person and the family. It will be very important to give this person pain killer so that he/ she can get rid of the painful condition.

Keep 3 to 4 packets of paracetamol in the first aid kit. But be sure to keep on revising the expiry date of the medicine so that you have the medicine with correct shelf life.

20.Antibiotics

The discovery of antibiotic has brought a revolution in the world of medicine. The diseases which were previously lethal were cured with efficiency. Since its discovery, it has been used to treat a variety of diseases.

They are also one of the essential parts of the emergency kit. They can be given to the people who may complain of diarrhea, fever or any other infection. You can easily administer them any broad spectrum antibiotic until the injured person is taken to the hospital where proper diagnosis and treatment can be done.

There are many varieties of antibiotics in the market. Choose some broad spectrum antibiotic that can kill a multitude of disease-causing agents. There are many websites and books that can give you a guideline about the name of the antibiotic and use. Take help from there and administer the antibiotic. This practice of random medication is not recommended in daily routine. It is just for an emergency situation.

Keep 3 to 4 packets of antibiotic in the first aid kit. But be sure to keep on revising the expiry date of the medicine so that you have the medicine with correct shelf life. Also keep a record of the drugs with which any of the family members has an allergy. You do not want to get involved in any extra trouble when it is an emergency.

The best place to keep these items is in a box as you do not want to run for the things that are scattered. Also keep it in a place that is accessible and can be accessed in case of any emergency. It is also important that every member of the family has the clear idea about the location of first aid kit. Keep the first aid kit in the kitchen as it is the place where there is less humidity. Increased humidity can cause a reduction in the shelf life of these items.

Chapter 05: Priceless Dirt-cheap Items for SHTF

Many of the supplies that are used for the prepping are expensive. Many of the people in case of SHTF will think to have dirt cheap items. This can be taken from an example that toilet paper is easily available in the market that is quite cheap. In the case of any SHTF, they become expensive and quite hard to find.

The use of dirt cheap items is necessary and they should be in stock so that they can be used later on. They can be bought at really cheap prices and can be used later on. Some of the dirt cheap items for SHTF are:

21. Toilet paper

The use of tissue paper is in every home. They are used in the toilet, rooms, and kitchen and for every kind of wiping. The most extensive use of this tissue paper is in the toilet where they are used on an extensive basis. It will be very economical if you buy these tissue papers in dirt cheap. It will not only be used in daily routine but also during any case of disaster and after SHTF.

There are many vendors who are supplying dirt cheap toilet paper with reasonable pricing and variety in quality. All you need to do is find the right vendor and get your hands on this toilet paper.

Keep bundles of toilet paper which you can use later on. They can be used in case of any disaster from cleaning and wiping till cleaning any blood. They will be used for maintenance of hygiene which is very necessary for the health of your family.

22.Soap

Soap is used in every home. It has many uses from bathing and washing to cleaning. There are many brands of soap in the market. There are bath soaps, dishwashing soaps, and cleaning soaps. They are very important for maintenance of hygiene of you and your family member.

All you need is to find the right vendor who can provide you with the right number and quality of soaps. You not only use it after SHTF but can be used in daily routine. It is imperative that you store a number of sizes, variety, and types of these soaps. You also do not need to worry about the shelf life of these plants as well.

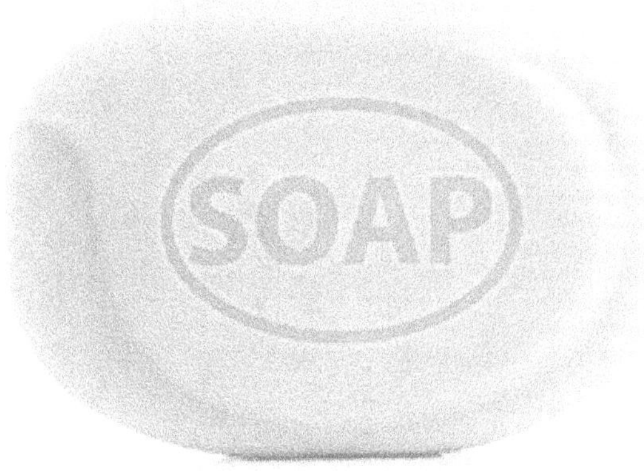

23.Ziploc bags

Ziploc bags are the plastic bags that are used to store anything anywhere. You can put any vegetable, fruit or any other food item and store it in the kitchen or the refrigerator.

They are also used to store other stuff like clothes, jewelry, buttons and any other thing that can be stored.

The use of Ziploc bags is many and uncountable. It will be very convenient if the Ziploc bags are bought in dirt cheap. You can use them to store items not only in the daily routine but also in a case of emergency. They are light weight, portable and easy to carry.

One of the other advantages is that you can easily see the stuff present in it. All you need is to find the right vendor who can provide you with the right number and quality of Ziploc bags. You not only use it after SHTF but can be used in daily routine. It is imperative that you store a number of sizes, variety, and types of these Ziploc bags. You also do not need to worry about the shelf life of these plants as well.

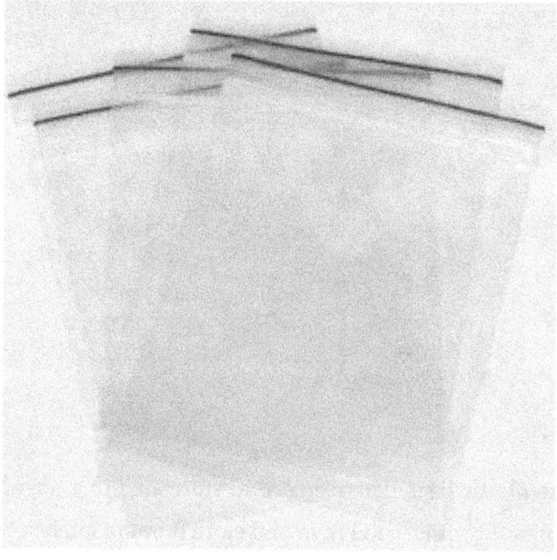

24.Candles

Candles are used in the daily routine being portable and easy tom use. We can find a lot of variety of this in the market. They can be bought in dirt cheap which can be used in daily life in many cases when there is a shortage of power supply or most importantly in the case of the nay disastrous condition.

It will be very convenient if you buy a good stock of these in dirt cheap and store them. It will not only be convenient but is also cheap. These candles can be used in case of disaster if the torches go down and there is no facility of batteries. You can easily light any candle and avail the advantage.

There are many vendors who are supplying dirt cheap candles with reasonable pricing and variety in quality. All you need to do is find the right vendor and get your hands on these candles.

25.Match sticks

Matches are the basic need in the kitchen. They are used on daily routine in the kitchen. They are used for lighting purpose. In the case of any emergency, the values of match stick are increased, and it gets hard to find it. To avoid such nuisance, you can buy bundles of matches from dirt cheap and store them.

It is important that you buy good quality of match sticks which are long. They have the advantage that they have unlimited shelf life. Make sure that you keep them away from humidity and fire.

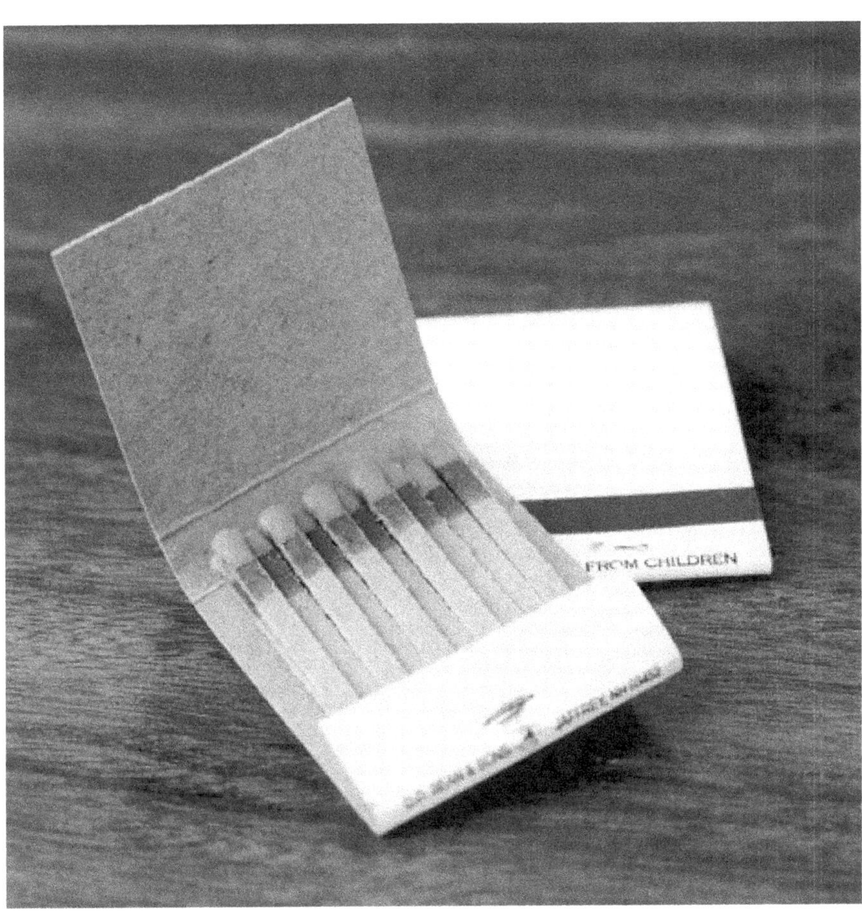
FROM CHILDREN

Conclusion

The book has given a thorough insight into the way in which people can prepare them by use of dirt cheap items and help them out of this situation. Disaster can inflict any one at any time. They do not come with any warning sign. It is necessary that we should be prepared for this situation. This preparation requires proper planning. The book has given a thorough insight into dealing with the situations in an effective manner. The book has given well oriented and well-groomed information for the readers. The readers will find this book easy to reads and understand. By following these simple techniques and strategies, you can save your family from harm. All you need to do is read this book with concentration and get the most out of it. In the end, I would like to thank the reader for downloading this book and read it.

FREE Bonus Reminder

If you have not grabbed it yet, please go ahead and download your special bonus E book *"Chakras for Beginners. 7 Steps To Understand And Balance Chakras, Radiate Energy, And Strengthen Aura"*.

Simply Click the Button Below

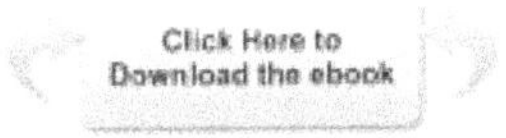

OR Go to This Page

http://lifehacksworld.com/free

BONUS #2: More Free & Discounted Books & Products

Do you want to receive more Free/Discounted Books or Products?

We have a mailing list where we send out our new Books or Products when they go free or with a discount on Amazon. Click on the link below to sign up for Free & Discount Book & Product Promotions.

=> Sign Up for Free & Discount Book & Product Promotions <=

OR Go to this URL

http://zbit.ly/1WBb1Ek

www.ingramcontent.com/pod-product-compliance
Lightning Source LLC
Chambersburg PA
CBHW050803240726

48654CB00008B/616